The
Backwaters
Press

THE BACKWATERS PRIZE IN POETRY

LONG RULES

An Essay in Verse

Nathaniel Perry

THE BACKWATERS PRESS   *An imprint of the University of Nebraska Press*

Acknowledgments for the use of copyrighted
material appear on pages 61–62, which
constitute an extension of the copyright page.

Library of Congress Cataloging-in-Publication Data
Names: Perry, Nathaniel Dixon, 1979– author.
Title: Long rules : an essay in
verse / Nathaniel Perry.
Description: [Lincoln] : The Backwaters Press, an
imprint of the University of Nebraska Press, [2021]
Series: The Backwaters Prize in Poetry
Identifiers: LCCN 2021012060
ISBN 9781496227980 (paperback)
ISBN 9781496229281 (epub)
ISBN 9781496229298 (pdf)
Subjects: BISAC: POETRY / Subjects & Themes /
Family | POETRY / Subjects & Themes /
Inspirational & Religious | LCGFT: Poetry.
Classification: LCC PS3616.E7936
L66 2021 | DDC 811/.6—dc23
LC record available at
https://lccn.loc.gov/2021012060

Set in Garamond Premier by Laura Buis.
Designed by N. Putens.

Frontispiece: *Sign*, Horatio Perry,
2020, pencil. Courtesy of author.

Welcome, Basil, my friend! Come, take thy place on the settle
Close by the chimney-side, which is always empty without thee

—Longfellow

CONTENTS

LONG RULES

I

Our Lady of the Angels

CROZET, VIRGINIA

Listen, child of God, to Willie Nelson
and the way he lives between the basic things
you can hear—or his voice lives there, I should say to be
precise, and we must try to be precise;
the voice and the body are not the same. The prayers
we fashion leave their cavities and rise
like anchorites hailing dawn from desert caves.
And though those anchorites have bodies proper,
in my metaphor they themselves have been
transmogrified into living prayers that fly
and live, like melodies, stretched across
the staves and stanzas of a living air;
and what in heaven's name are they doing there?
Clustered inside themselves, they've emptied their selves.
The desert fathers could turn their backs to the dying
day and stand toward the east then not
sit down until dawn defined their darkened faces
(and what had grown behind their faces) again.
They thought only of Christ, who was for them
like Willie Nelson's voice, inhabiting
not only Adam's ribs, but the meaty spaces

between them, and the hours between lauds
and compline and the grains of sand between
their sandals and their feet. And then there's Basil
of Caesarea, young student turned monk and turned
again to bishop as he tried to build
belief from place and place from people, who knew
spirit and man and god to be the same,
who in his letters condemns alike revenge
and fancy sandals. But to my mind, the sand
caught up in any shoe is more or less
the same, a mild and reminding pain you wouldn't
know about until you know it's there,
and you suddenly complain, which is like prayer:
the voice and body separate and make
a sound. And come to think of it, the prayer,
the sentence said, the lullaby, the letter
read out loud, the song, the hail, the welcome
and wail unwound are a sort of spirit, not pure,
but plain human sound that's got the sand still in it.
It was the time of the preacher when the story began—
you can almost feel it running through your hands.

❖

I was humming that repeating and opening
melody from *Red Headed Stranger* for no
clear reason as I drove very slowly down
the four-mile gravel road I'd gotten on
the wrong end of as I headed toward Our Lady
of the Angels in Crozet. I passed a dairy
called Tucked-Away where huge oaks had been tossed
like pick-up sticks in winds the week before.
Every hundred yards or so a clearing
would remind me of the mountains. Clustered inside
themselves, they'd emptied their selves and made new storms,
which flashed and complained in a low familiar accent
as I got to the part in the song where the lesson begins
and turned down the monastery's crusher run drive.
I had come in from the far wrong end of Clark Road
because I thought the bridge was out, or I
assumed, when I looked at the map and saw a creek
and got to the road and saw the orange sign
that warned me that the road was closed somewhere down
its line, that where it would be out would be
the bridge. That it wasn't out was my main lesson
for the day, and the young nun I passed when I
was leaving looked at me as if I should
have known the crossing was fine. In the chapel I sat
alone and looked at where they put the wine
for mass, and the comb-bound psalm books worn by hands
and hands at compline. *Through my fault, through
my fault*, the laminated prayer card said.

I put my head in my hands to listen, and what
I heard was the murmuring of air-conditioning
(St. Benedict loathed a murmurer, though didn't
know this kind) and the mantra of refrigerator
compressors from adjacent rooms. They make
cheese here, I remembered, and suddenly realized
that these intrusive sounds were the breathing of
the place—no cheese, no work; no work, no self;
no self, no prayer; no prayer, no god; no river,
no bridge to bridge from there to there. I stood
and left the noisy chapel and went back out
to ring the bell for cheese. The sister who took
my check told me please to keep the Gouda cold
and to eat it even when it starts to mold.

❖

Basil is no model of restraint.
It's Benedict, to remind you, who wrote
the rules that later gave us Trappist beer
and our image of Silence and the sense that one
private life could serve as an unknown goodness
in the world. Basil was full-throttle caught up in
the world, moaning in letters that his city
had been cronied into ruin, that his sideman
Dorotheus was pious enough for two
messengers and could convince any number
of bishops that he, Basil, the author, in a sense,
of the Holy Spirit as we know it, was right
about things theological and things
theosophical and things theo-
political, etc. But Basil
knew community and what it brings to selves—
that clustered inside ourselves, we empty the self
from the body, that the self is natively
alone, but the body needs neighbors to shiver through
the winter with and bend down next to in
the fields. The body wields the self and the self
the body, and then the voice, as Basil knows
so clearly in the media of public
and private letters. Though his endgame is to break
this earthly trinity, wanting *the severance
of the soul from sympathy with the body*, he senses
it only will come with death. To Gregory
he writes, prefiguring Emerson, that in

his *out-of-the-way place* he has not been able,
yet, to *leave himself behind*. And he never will.
He sends the self astride the voice in every
letter sent and gets it back with those received.
Though he's pleased with his attempts at solitude—
who hasn't felt warm and sweetly sacred in
a cultivated quiet, our burnished beings-
alone? The Christian monk has his eye always
on God, but God, in turn, is looking down
and back at the way and where we all sit down
in the world—the way the roadside blackberries
are ripening at different rates along
our roads, for instance, the way the deer we live
among are somehow constant and elusive.

❖

The sister I talked to when I bought my round
of cheese told me that in work, she thinks,
she finds herself. I think the same old thing
I told her, and she looked as if she couldn't
figure out exactly what sort of work I might
do, but she smiled and nodded and smiled again
when I said the place and the mountains especially
were beautiful and overshadowing
in the way you want things over you, and she
said, yes, the setting is a blessing. I wondered,
then, if a blessing, too, can be a setting,
if the land is some asked-for graceful prayer made real
around us. Who prayed it up? And who is keeping
it going? On my way out of the monastery, I put
a slip of paper in the prayer box asking
"a prayer for the land that surrounds us" just in case
it needed a little extra boosterism
from these quiet quarters. The sun outside
had made a prism of every bit of water
that the storm had mustered up and painted
on the leaves of fire maples along the drive.
Clustered inside themselves, the drops of water
lost themselves to the bright watery light.
I walked down to the little circle in
the driveway meant for Sunday worshipers
to park their cars, and I still could hear the quiet
and the less quiet sounds of sisters moving
through the early summer open windows facing

the road. A blessing is a place to sit
and watch in for a while, the blue-gray bulk
of the Blue Ridge behind me like pairs of hands raised up,
we guess, in praise. Here, in the *quiet, little
out-of-the-way place* they've made, lives make.
Willie Nelson is no model of restraint,
but in singing he holds us back, and to the deals
the melody has made. When the lovers dance
with their smiles on their faces, the chord changes before
they do, the bright city lights shine out in the setting
of a simple tune, the basic fall and rise
again of the land, of the sound of the land, of storms
above the doings of women and men, who bless
each other: always, until, entire, unless.

❖

"Can I Sleep in Your Arms?"—a cover, and the old
unanswered question of anyone of faith.
The Benedictine tradition has its adherents,
during the Great Silence after compline,
ask more or less that exact thing of Christ,
wondering if they can surrender their selves in one
more way. Basil was willing to give himself.
In fact one recurring feature of his letters
is his always worsening health and the way it creeps
higher and higher up in the saying of what
he has to say to friends and colleagues alike.
But he was not ready to sacrifice his town,
the community he'd built on the model of giving
away the self. Groups of holy people,
groups of people, whole, for him, are something
like the Trinity—mysterious unity,
strange and meaningful separations. Clustered,
but still inside our selves, we make a clearer
self, he might have said. Our voices singing
out together do not lose their character
but have a different tamber, a quality
without a name. One mountain on a plain
is a disconcerting thing, not like a range,
which gives of its topography and makes
an entirety of place. In Crozet, Our Lady
of the Angels sits on a down-sloping field.
Its musty pew-crowded waiting room of a chapel
looks out as if from the mountains, as if to be

in a place, in a way, is to create the place,
as if a living winging prayer were made
reanimate inside us, something physical
I mean, like a new cell or a tiny hermit
in our heart-caves, every time we see a place,
and begin again to draw the world around
our bodies. As I left the monastery to go
back to town and find my family,
a pregnant doe walked so casually across
the road, I felt like I was crossing her
road home instead. I stopped and looked as far
down the deer path as I could. The animal
was gone and had left, except in me, no mark.
I kept a little vigil there, until dark.

II

Holy Cross Abbey

BERRYVILLE, VIRGINIA

Listen, child of God, to the sound of the wind
in the trees; it is everywhere around us, a river
we cannot climb to but would surely drown
in if we could. *I lift my eyes to the mountains,*
sings the psalm, and I could see the mountains from there,
like a hand held to the face for slow inspection,
but I didn't need the hills to hear the wind.
It played the branches like a dulcimer—
and fence rails and gravestones and the half-ripe grains
of field grass and road weed that lined the driveway I drove
down to the abbey of the Holy Cross.
Hay was baled off and on into the horizon,
which was baled into the mountains that surround
the abbey and its grounds in a horseshoe of rise
and fall. The monks don't make the hay, I know
(they make fruitcakes and little tubs of spun honey),
but the rhythm of any tended grassland seems
an apt environment—there's more or less
a time to cut, then dry, then rake, then dry
and bale and carry off; and when there's rain
everyone has too much, and when the summer's

dry there's never anywhere enough.
A singer I almost knew, a friend of a friend
of course, who seems himself a monk of sorts
in his songs (though in his life too lost too long
to qualify by Basil's or Benedict's
conformations), wanted to know before
he died of trying not to fail, *how can
I be the only one, whose life can't live
up to the light?* and I thought to myself as the hay
became woods and then a guest house and then the abbey,
that it is our native sense of loneliness
that drives us all not only back into
ourselves but also to communities
of solitude. What is marriage if not
sitting in a house's rooms at night
at ease with hardly speaking? What are friends
if not always far away? The light, there,
was bright and voices leaked through the hot afternoon
like wind from windows as I walked toward
the chapel, where the midday prayer would start at two.
I had ten minutes and didn't know what to do.

❖

There's something about Basil's fourteenth letter
that stops everyone who ever gets
that far into early Christian monastic arcana.
He describes, for the only time, and to his friend
Gregory (not his famous mystic brother
of the same name), the geographical
situation of where he would begin
to try to touch the god he'd read about.
What he doesn't say to Gregory here
is that a younger brother also tried
his hand at touching God in that same place
and died there fishing, caught up in the nets
and onrush of spring waters with the same
blank hills looking on. Basil tells his friend,
in the Loeb translation of course, *There is a high
mountain covered with a thick forest,
watered on its northerly side by cool
and transparent streams*. He says with its woods and waters
and limited roads it is *by no means far
from being an island*, which is a good description
of my own nine acres and of this Blue Ridge
and river-ringed monastery not fifty miles
from DC. And what I'm insinuating there, too,
is key for Basil in his rural seat,
that the distance of the city is one of the great
fruits he can harvest in that place. While I
prefer the blackberries and butternut squash
I squeeze from my own Calypso's isle, I think

we know what he was getting at—that only in
retreat does solitude seem meaningful.
But is that true? or had Basil not yet grasped
that tranquility, as Thoreau once figured out,
comes in the tumultuous company
of deer and spiders and cowpea curculios
and children and yellow-necked caterpillars
and water striders and Carolina wrens
and white-tailed rabbits and groundhogs going down
into the ground and ground squirrels and pigweed and dogs
and tree frogs and the moon? Those are my
nonsolitudes. Basil could have had
his own litany of company, could have played
it like a dulcimer his lord had made.

❖

How can I be the only one whose heart
refuses to try? the song goes on. Not
as good as the line before it, I'll admit,
but a reasonable sentiment for any-
one who's stopped for any length of time
to think about their love and whether it
is adequate to what it finds itself
in service to—a child, a wife, a father,
a god, a meadow filled with clover blossom,
old dogs, another child, etc.
The monks at Holy Cross must feel that way
about these mountains and the mountain shadows
that slide down, as if from the sky, upon them.
Could you even try to meet such a gesture halfway?
I climbed the stairs to the chapel just before
the hour and sat alone in the long room,
which looks like the inside of a capsized boat,
tongue-and-groove ceiling with mistakes along the trim,
and it occurred to me that the line in the song might be
how can I be the only one whose life
can't live up to the lie? not light, but before
I could sing it quietly to myself to figure
which version might be right, the brothers appeared
and began to find their ways to pews along
the walls of the boat, I mean chapel, bowing each
and each in their own predetermined manner
to the crucifix fixed to the wall at the bow of the room.
They come, as the reader of Benedict's Rule would know,

immediately from whatever they might
have been doing—the bell rings out and plays them like
a dulcimer, still strings tuned toward prayer,
which that day was psalm, scripture, some standing up
and sitting down, a plea against the devil's
devilry and silence. And in that silence
was also the ambiguity of the words
I can't remember—there is light and there are lies,
and there are mountains and the taller ones behind
them. And speaking of light, I could barely make out
the sun through the skinny windows on the port
wall, though there were no lights on in the room.
The monks filed out haphazardly, to starboard,
and the day sailed on toward earth's own upturned harbor.

❖

Sorting out the ins and outs of Basil's rules
is not easy; what have been known as the Long Rules
are really the first section of his *Asketikon*,
a work he revised into its final form
when he was named bishop of his birthplace.
The Rule of St. Basil is the Latin translation
of a first draft of that same *Asketikon*,
whose Greek original is lost. Benedict
and other directors of Western solitude
had that Latin text, but the Long Rules contain
much of the same material and are
more conversational and more controversial
(some maintain they were revised and even written
whole cloth by others), but in all of this,
in drafts and versions and also in his letters,
there's Basil spending a life defining the quiet
of life lived in communion with other lives
and with a thing they will never see but know
and know. I won't go into the feisty mess
of late fourth-century theopolitics,
but Basil supported the Nicene Creed, which means
he believed the spirit and the son and his God
were all the same, none subordinated
to the other, and none *made*, just there, which means,
if you follow, that Basil believed what is never wasn't,
and in a word, in mystery. He needed
mystery to believe. In fact, he was never
really interested in making sense of what

he knew as mystery but saw in it
a model—men and women, communities,
were also something like a mystery.
To be alone, a hermit, is, in a way,
a selfish thing. True solitude, the knowledge
of the self within the self can only come
from self within a world and in the bargains
made with others. A single string plucked
just rings and rings and rings and rings but makes
no harmony. Basil played community
like a dulcimer, something simple but full of every
possible interval. An octave, if played
exactly, *seems* almost one note only—a question
and answer together sound a single suggestion.

❖

And Basil's rules are simply that: a series
of questions and responses (where Benedict
makes topical pronouncements). Now I'm not weighing
in for any one tradition, or even one
religion, but a question implies communion,
a group figuring out together how to be
alone in the rushing spirit-rivers coursing
the world. A river plays along the road
that leads to Holy Cross like a hand along
a dulcimer, and in any real rain the road
would flood and the monks wouldn't be the only cloistered
things in Berryville. The world we make
is not the world. The things we find ourselves holding
are sometimes all we can hold. Before I left
the monastery I visited the gift shop,
where I bought some honey and a handful of books.
I chatted with the brother running the shop,
and he was sardonic and grumpy when I asked
if he'd been to Gethsemani, said he didn't want
to go, had heard it was too hot in Kentucky.
He rang up my books on an iPad, and the total came
out high, but I paid and left and walked back out
into the light, which was just beginning to make
its evening acquaintance with the tops of oaks
and the mountains supervising things behind them.
The light asks a simple question and shadows respond;
no one should forgive me, I knew what I stood
to lose—that song again. Its walled words

right or wrong, the song and the world it was sung
into are both a kind of gospel and
the blues all in one. Song and world and words
all something we have lost, or still are losing;
every year winter takes our fat sweet things
away; the line trees we like to think are straight
ladders up to heaven come down in light
rain. *That simple old tune on the stage each night
marking the time I lost you*, that's some lost office
of hours to be sure. I walked to my car
and heard voices from the monastery hallways
like wind chase July's shadows down the drive,
which chased me, as I backed out, slanting quick black sleet
through the windshield and across my car's empty seats.

III

Mepkin Abbey

MONCKS CORNER, SOUTH CAROLINA

Listen, child of God, to the saddle-backed
caterpillar chewing on blueberry leaves,
but don't put your ear too close. I've tried, just after
they've stung me twice and twice again while picking
August berries. They don't look at you, because
you can't see them looking, but you suspect they're looking
at you and laughing some kind of inside laugh,
which stems from the complicated realization
of a great species-wide joke about caution
and sweetness and the inability
of the human eye to register danger. I don't
find it funny, but I am not a caterpillar.
And, of course, the moth they morph into for a few
sky-filled weeks is unremarkable,
so this is all they have—some poison and
some laughs and half of one of my blueberry plants.
There's something in the care they take devouring
every leaf they light upon that is so like
a saint, like Basil and how in letters he praises
the widows he knows will never love again
and tears up every man he thinks has ever

even thought of questioning the rightness or
the wrongness of the creeds his troubled branch
of Christians has subscribed to—the moth should fly
to the light like every other moth. Thomas
Merton, even in his first famous
book, complains of having little time,
by the time he is well-established as a monk,
for contemplation, that all he's asked to do
is teach and write and write and work. Like Basil,
he was the face of an idea, and like
the caterpillars, he'd spent, by then, all
his surprises on the world, and what was left
was the balm and the poisons you'd expect. At least
that's how he seemed to see it then. You spend
your time stretching for something, and then it seems
the stretching, not the something, was what you needed.
I tend the row of Japanese turnips I've never
grown before with intense care; I'm on
my knees for the in-row weeding, but when they come in,
their dull gold globes clustered in huge paws,
I'm stymied. I only know to eat them raw.

❖

I bet they don't grow these turnips in Moncks Corner,
where Mepkin Abbey sits cowled in Spanish moss
and nearly choked in the embrace of the wide
Cooper River. It's just too warm down here
for the cold root tang of the turnip, at least in spring.
But they do grow mushrooms and rent their fields for cotton
and beans, and they used to keep chickens on a surprising
scale. The place has the feel of a half-defunct
country club, whose members stay mostly hidden
from view. There's a pole barn with a concrete roof,
which in itself seems impossible, but then
the roof is shaped like a row of turnip roots,
like some kind of Hindu temple on stilts with a cross
stuck on top lest you get confused. It is, in short,
a wonder of contemplative architecture.
It is kind of like the face of an idea
that's not voiced too often in a place like this,
that strangeness and surprise might be the bedrock
of faith, if faith is comfort in what you don't know
or understand, which it is, at least in the hands
that hold it most convincingly. The docents
here, volunteers from Charleston, tour you through
immaculate beds of native annuals
and half-tropical perennials and shrubs
and vines that snake up and around the trees like tape
pulled loose from its winding. They are pious about the place.
In the chapel, at midday prayer, the volunteers
and visitors listen to the brothers sing

while looking to the roof as if for something
that is no longer there. But the place is there
in a way no faith can tangibly be. Can you
hear me? I whispered to the river bend
choked with lilies and marshweed and the silt
from rice islands dredged by slaves a century
and a half ago, and I'm pretty sure it heard;
I'm pretty sure I heard it singing a country
gospel tune I know, *we're gonna shout,*
we're gonna shout, everybody will be happy
over there, and it seemed convinced, though it's not clear
if *over there* was heaven or just the brush-run
island I saw risen in the river,
with its low earthly version of forever.

❖

I think it is more than safe to assume that Basil
would not agree with the room for error implied
by the tune I'm calling up here. Everybody
will *not* be happy because most folks will not
be going over there. So much of Basil's
midlife output has to do with chalk-dry,
pick-up-sticks, who-and-why doctrine,
which other trembling members of the faithful
have asked him once again to clarify.
In the same moral breath he bans abortion
but excuses the ever-unintentional murder
of a servant with the lash. That the loving lord
will not wash all sins away, it seems, is a sword
that cuts both ways to my mind sitting now
in the front-wake clarifying sun of a morning
that is suddenly September as summer ashes
over. This light, this threshold-making spider
light of after-dawn, is like a rule.
It makes community of whatever it touches
and leaves, at times, even good things in the shadows,
which collect and pool at the margins of the yard.
Who lives there, Basil? Would you let them in? Whoever
knocks on the door of the monastery can enter,
but there are so many unforgiveable sins . . .
One can only read the hair-splitting of doctrinal
carping for so long, but in it is something
desperate and familiar—that we must know who
we are to know who we are. We require a sense

of the light to know its shining on us. In his
more private moments Basil knows this is
not exactly right. Light is something constant
and something constantly elusive. The moon,
when sought, says Emerson in a sober moment,
is *mere tinsel*, but when felt as a presence, a rule
you didn't write, it is beautiful, the face
of an idea not divinable
by tractate or sermon or by the widest eye
or our shallow topographies of nerves. Now what
we know in syllables we can know in the soul,
but the soul makes up rules, I'll warn you, as it goes
along, which make, themselves, for a kind of song,
like a caterpillar's chewing; and it's long.

❖

The album I know that song from is also called
Everybody Will Be Happy Over There
and is a local recording of a church's
bluegrass band, from Vinton, Virginia. I found
it in a thrift store. The group is Strings of Praise,
and they are better than you might expect—
the harmonies are clean, the banjo player
good, his Gibson resonator's moonlike
body on the cover like an eye
in the face of everyone's idea of heaven.
On the LP's cover the sky is also weirdly
white. There are pines and the singers' clothes do not
suggest a season. The band is smiling, gathered
on a railroad track, as if they'd like to hustle
on *over there* at the hands of the Norfolk Southern.
But they're not going anywhere until
they've tied their voices, at least, together to stay.
And here this unknown gospel group has come
to mind in the most unlikely of places, a Trappist
monastery in South Carolina. Though monks
have voices too, and in their rural chapel
they're as inaccessible as harmonies
filed away in a thrift-store record bin.
Who can ever tell where our voices will go?
I sat in the pews with the brothers during midday
prayer and ate my lunch with retreatants and guests
in the refectory. I knew most
of the prayers and melodies just from my scant

neighborliness with the Episcopal Church
as a child, but in the same way I can't play
the banjo right (my fingers lift exactly
when they shouldn't), I couldn't sing along.
In fact, I left lunch early by mistake,
thinking the prayers and silence were done, when in fact
they had just begun. I stood outside the windows
of the room I had just been in and watched
other people pray. It began to rain
a little, but not in a romantic way
or with the melodrama you'd want the image
to end on. It just rained a short hot while as it does
in South Carolina and stopped. I went back in,
wanting only to know if the prayers would end.

❖

Back on the turnips; they are good enough to plant
again for fall, but often only a few
come up—cutworms being so much worse
in August than in March, the sun less willing
to light the lees and corners we have for land
for long enough. But turnips are tough. Their one
root swells and sweetens through the falling year.
I've learned there's no real need to thin them, they like
to touch, like biscuits in a pan. They fatten
then bend at angles complementary
to the widening circumferences of friends.
The brothers at Mepkin Abbey sit close in the chapel
pews, mouthing silent and spoken prayers, the air
rapid with words and the paddle blade of psalms
sung in unison. The river appreciates
a community of solitude, I think—
herons rising from the woods, folded in flight
like a carpenter's ruler, stubborn fish hiding
in creases of reedy light below them. The heron
does not speak to the river, but their voices
join in song: *we will hear nobody praying and no*
mourning in that land; mothers, fathers, sisters,
brothers. Everybody will be happy over
there. In heron-air, in human prayer,
in turnip-tang and flair, in river-where,
in Basil's healthless graceful word-made care,
in notes the banjo and the guitar share,
the song shimmers like a face, or the face

of an idea, at least, of what we mean
by communion. My Basil and Merton, both divested
or less burdened, would sigh and help me to the altar
of my choosing. At Mepkin Abbey there are signs
around the grounds showing visitors
the lines past which only the brothers can pass.
There are no words, just a cartoon monk without
a face and his hand held out. I like to think
he's not keeping me out or even pointing
some way in. But instead he's asking me
to read his palm, the lines his solitude
(made within the hands of others) has drawn.
And we should read those things, letters left, a hand,
a banjo's face, without needing to understand.

IV

Our Lady of Gethsemani

NEW HAVEN, KENTUCKY

Listen, child of God, to the rain riding
bareback over the knobs. I could see its shadow,
or the gray-shift light of moving downpour that made
a figure like a shadow, coming in.
Knobs are what they call the little hills
in the stretch of central Kentucky near New Haven
where the abbey of Gethsemani
sits beside its parking lot with a Spanish
kind of grace—pools of shade, white walls,
the quiet you'd expect a quiet place
to make. I came with my friend M to swim
and eat and talk with one of the brothers he knows,
who studied under Merton here and has prayed
in one place through more than fifty years of war—
and more than fifty years of wild petunias
shrugging through the weed grass, beehives sweeting
split-holes in the oaks, ironwood trees
forgetting their given names, black raspberries
each year by the roadsides resharpening old thorns.
Without my glasses in the pond, I listened
to the woodpeckers embroidering the trees

and marveled at their constant sense of alarm.
I treaded water half an hour straight
with thunder in the distance and the dark uncaring
cold of collected water all around me,
with no alarm. M and I at vespers
felt no alarm, though the day was dying its first
little bit, and when we rode away from the chapel
for dinner, we tried hard to whittle our silence
down by shouting over the Gator's engine,
which Brother P bounced hard along the broken
road. We ate where Thomas Merton tried
to keep his later years, a hermitage
of cinder blocks, white paint, a skinny altar
and one room big enough to gather in.
Here, his desert fathers and pre-Confucians
and saints and brothers gathered in the air,
and other monks and friends and strangers might
have come and been together in the chairs.
We sat on the small porch with cold quiche and beer
and talked about calm and worry and their shared shores,
and the woodpeckers at the pond and the sycamores.

❖

Basil also filled his days with alarm,
and come to think of it, he was not unlike
a woodpecker, the cold of collected water
somewhere always beneath his voice but worry
sounding out above. His letters are
a long and looping story, a hodgepodge of doctrine
and veiled emotion, as I've mentioned before,
but also of defense. Basil puts his armor
up notably in a letter from the summer
of 375 about *the singing of psalms*,
defending in particular the way
his people had come to sing them—in antiphons,
the call and response enacting what one never
can expect from prayer. But by dawn, they all would be
in common, as of one voice and one heart with somehow
still *each one forming his own expression*
of repentance. They're two, then one, then they are many,
solitude a room inside community,
if you want to put it another way, like a mine
inside a mountain. And I mean some careful kind
of mine, not the strip mines and beheadings John Prine
sang about more than forty years ago
in "Paradise," which is not antiphonal
but does have notable harmony in its famous
chorus, where Paradise itself is lost
inside the past, the memory of God
(writ green) destroyed by men and their pagan machines,
or that at least is how Basil might have heard it.

He certainly would have thought of his own first try
at a quiet life—that home-place in the same
sweet-valley green of grace his brother had lived
and later died in, *where the air smelled like snakes*,
or probably did. He would have also thought
about his family's land in Neocaesarea,
which he loved for *the quiet of its solitude*,
and its distance from the *troubles of civic life*.
But Basil, like Prine, knew better. Life arrows
its way into every retreat—in letters and lignite,
carbon and cross. Solitude, then, is a living
memory of the places we lose, and every
place we live in, of course, is already lost,
evening shadows the shadow of an absented host.

❖

Not far from Gethsemani, a handful of counties
to the south, the Green River ends in a fingerwork
of creeks, three hundred miles away from where
it carves out Mammoth Cave and waters mines
and works its way through TVA dams. John Prine
thought heaven lay just beyond the third of the dams,
though that may have been a figure of speech, given
that strip-mining had by then, 1971,
when the record was released, scabbed its way
along the whole western course of the river
where the cold of collected water could only cast
reproving glances as it filled with silt.
Not a figure of speech, I guess, but a figure of trust.
Contemplative monks are seen by their churches as keepers
of liturgical hours—those who toe the ancient
rites of observance, who are up for matins,
on watch at vigils, who manage the management
of time for God for others—conservationists
in the strictest sense—keeping something so others
might know it is kept. In the same way singing a song
like "Paradise" doesn't keep anything unspoiled
(harmonizing drunk with your friends, then adding
a banjo in), knowing monks are praying
doesn't keep things right, but they say it's something
we can point to, and constant things deserve
a pointing to—immigrant honeysuckle
inebriating the air, sinkholes sinking
into what rock is no longer there, crawdads

shedding rust-ruby shells and claws, ticks testing
laws of grasses and wind, the jewelweed's bend
beside the poison ivy of a creek bank.
And though we love to drape the natural world
in monkish robes of our own desire for quiet,
these, too, are hours kept in concert, a system
of plain action that looks to us like peace.
Brother P sang the liturgy at vespers
in a simple practiced quaver that climbed up over
the brothers' voices, climbed up out of the mine
and then dove down again, into the region
where we hope the spirit can be parceled out
and used. *Let my soul roll on up to the Rochester Dam,*
not yet, of course, he meant in course, when it can.

❖

There's an irony in Basil's being kept
alive largely by his letters (his writings,
remember, went through so many translations
and transformations, he is hard to find
at times). In a letter to a man whose name
is Hilarius (I know, I know), he states
his preference for meeting face to face.
He writes, *the living word makes for more*
effective persuasion, and it is not, he adds,
like the written word, open to attack
and subject to calumny. Though later in
that same letter he describes himself
as one of *those who have studied human weakness*,
a phrase so delicate, even translated,
you wonder if it would have come around
at all in conversation, or if it needed
to be written down to live like that in the mind,
the way cold collects in the cold of collected water.
Monks, after Basil, were often copyists,
and there is something in Basil's letters that feels
like a mind being copied and recopied.
Right things are said in different ways, truths
resaid and tended to like lies. We prize
the sudden voice and its intensity
of lonely knowledge, but aren't the things we really
know inside the things we do again?
A letter might be read a dozen times
before it's put away, the song will sing

itself in a thousand voices when a guitar
is near. I've yet to meet a person who plays
the guitar and doesn't know most of "Paradise."
It's repeated, recrafted, the mines redug and ruined
again, but the spirit inside is each time refined.
When Basil denies, for the hundredth time, his role
in the heresies rumbling through Byzantium,
the solitude within his sense of faith
solidifies. He makes sense of himself to himself
when explaining himself to others. Our places become
our places when they start to change. The grapevine
that dies, when remembered, makes a new kind of fruit:
the disposition of the soul itself,
a book of letters, half-read, but still on the shelf.

❖

I mentioned beehives before, and M, at his house
a county over from Gethsemani,
showed me one he's been trying to catch. The hive
is well established in an oak, but he's put
a frame box on a nearby stump, ready
if the robber bees come in or when
a new queen needs to divide the colony.
It is, you could say, a forced sort of under-
standing of community, but honey
is one of those true sweet things, like correspondence,
that can't be made alone. At the hermitage
that night we rushed through dinner so Brother P
could get to compline, but we did have time
to compare our solitudes. I only knew M,
so I asked the others where they were from and realized
again how everyone's story is sometimes the same.
Like Basil we are all alone and sick,
but lonely stories seen together link
like landscape. When you cultivate solitude
alone, you are alone. When your solitude
is shared, your sickness in ways becomes a prayer,
one that asks whatever god is there
if not to answer then to understand
the context. Basil begs his friends to remember
that not only has he lived alone and felt
some holy spirit in his weakening bones,
but that he has always shared his loneliness,
his careful understanding of *human weakness*,

so that he, and others, might understand the human
part of that. Brother P told me he liked the way
Basil sees his rule as the answers to honest
questions: every morning the answer to honest sleep,
each meal the answer to an honest hunger.
The creek that runs by M's little greenhouse, its currents
and rapids reworking the cold of collected water
back into a narrative, surely finds
its way somehow to the Green River, the way
another soul leads you back into your own,
or how a song can take you to its source.
I remember seeing in M's house two guitars,
cases stacked and quiet on the living room floor,
paradise on either side of every door.

V

Cumberland County, Virginia

Listen, child of God, to the rare cool
of a July morning. And here I mean listen
to what isn't there—the curdle and whoop of heat-frogs,
the black-nosed white noise of compressor fans,
the almost whisper kiss of dry-dirt daisies
folding their leaves against the early sun,
morning-ventured rabbits on the run.
Though it's only barely middle summer, I
can just begin to feel fall shining up
its walking boots and laundering its robes,
like some Byzantine letter messenger
bringing back the frightening answers to summer's
long sun-drunk questions on the clarity
of certain points of doctrine. Fall doesn't think
it's funny the way the killdeer carry on,
or how the pigweed rams its radish root
into the soil like a skinny fist. The questions
on my long list keep coming back unanswered.
Like, who are we to care for other people?
Who am I to care about the shifting color
of the sky? Or are the colors shifting just

for me? I know that on the lower level,
the level of what I know empirically,
the level of the letter or the ringing
phone, I will never know—but maybe in
a glimpse of rayed light through morning trees,
or the frayed but good goodness in the space
between two people, between the notes of a song?
I'll listen to every song you know; I will clap
when you are through, Kelly Joe Phelps sings
in a song I love, a song like a letter read
again and again, a clapping like the applause
you'd give to the killdeer for his triple dive,
to the chickadee for his sung-out self-satisfaction,
to the owl I dreamed about, a barred owl, flying
down and singing at the same time, which I
do not think they do. But in my dream
it did, and when I woke I marveled again
at the beauty my mind and the world it mines and reshuffles
had accidentally made. And you, real world,
finish this early song with a cadence of dew
and lifting shadow; *maybe then I will kiss you.*

❖

Kiss the world. That's hilarious to think about.
I thought about kissing a wolf spider perched on top
of the first and biggest melon in the patch,
as a kind of protest to our base concepts
of ugliness and fear, but I gave in
to those very concepts, and anyway she ran
when my hand neared to check the cracks in the stem.
I kissed my wife on the back of the neck instead
when I came inside without the melon (it seemed
to need another day), and I thought that that
was close enough to the spider and to the world
to count as following through—not that anyone
was checking up on me, unless god counts thoughts
as contracts, which I don't think he's got time to do.
Basil would have counted a thought as a contract
if he had had a way of recording thought,
but all he had were semiprivate letters
and conversations and the memory
of friendships he had lost to faith, or to
the way faith is always misconstrued as fact.
Basil's insistence on the Trinity
as equal iterations of the same god,
and not three different things, suggests to me
that at the heart of the human community,
at the level of what we know empirically,
is a towering singular aloneness—that god
is the first example of solitude, but one
that only makes sense when embraced and sung and adorned

by a community of people who see themselves
in some fundamental way as always alone,
though striving to make spiritual the way
they see and understand their loneliness.
Like what a single zinnia in August would say
if it could talk instead of bow in the wind.
Basil had no way of knowing that in the end
his defense of oneness would seem so obvious
to the course of things in the West, and god only knows
what's right or real or whatever the word would be.
The one of the many of the one, that's close.
The one of the many of the one. I'm trying
to convince myself the way Basil might have done,
to tell myself the spider shouldn't have run.

❖

Come along to the riverside, sit down
now. I just want to hear somebody else whine,
Phelps sings at the beginning of that song—
as if that was what rivers were for, not absolution
but recitation, like I could shout down in
the hole a turnip makes when I pull it out
and tell the summer-deep spring what's on my mind,
and maybe my voice would sound out like a claxon
from a turnip hole two counties away, and someone
would make a poem, or a song, from the sorrows they hear,
which aren't really sorrows, I suppose, so much
as observations on the senselessness
of things, or fears. There are tears and holes in most
of the shirts I wear to work in the vegetables,
but they are not signs of suffering. I have not
suffered in notable ways, but every day
I've lived through has died just the same, priest-bats
breaking and drowning the wafer of the sun,
four-o'clocks closing on silent cue, the blue
of the starred starboard sky like a stain that's run.
At the level of what I know empirically,
there's sadness in every story, every dawn destroyed
by time, every man and woman framed by skin
and bone and therefore ever alone. But in
the monastery of the body, the mind
keeps a kind of watch, I think, like owls,
or mules, or, in the spring, a whip-poor-will.
The body makes the motions of loneliness,

the observed hours of waking and eating and grasping
and waving, while the mind watches and approves
or disapproves, we sometimes never know.
Though the mind does approve of outside offerings:
the turnip's creamy white, the starlike negative
blue of blueberries gone random ripe.
We band together in families to share
these sorts of things. In the monastery time
makes of this place, or any place a life
is lived, it is the community that marks
the solitudes without and within. The body
to the mind, the family to the bigger thing
behind the woodpeckers and chicory,
that god's-eye blue sometimes all you can see.

❖

I've been wondering why Basil is the one
whose voice has molehilled up so often here;
why not Benedict or Merton or the Little Flower
or Gregory or Cassian or King?
There's something there that's unremarkable
in the best of ways—a sparrow's nest before
a waterfall, a crow in his steadfast song.
The living of a life inside its walls
is long, but when the slightest variations
and turns in the established patterns make
a melody across the staves of days,
we can't help but try to pick it out with our pens,
or on a banjo, or with our kids, or friends.
Basil, in a later letter to the monks
at his monastery near Caesarea,
says he hopes they do not come to *favor*
the life that lacks witnesses, that *strictness*
of life in itself is not enough. He knows
that inside all the dreams of solitude
we have, even at the level of what we know
empirically, we can't see ourselves alone,
for a self is only a self in context, borders
only borders with something pressing in.
Landscape gets lost in the later set of letters,
no sign of the rushing river and watchful cradle
of hills from Basil's youth, but one senses a sense
of home in the letters—he's often regretting his illness
and subsequent inability to travel,

and beneath the apology is always the sound
of someone content with the place he's anchored in.
When you have slept and lived for long enough
in a single place, you learn the way alone
is never alone and the way the place becomes
a part of the body's landscape—what Hopkins had
as something more complicated-sounding than that,
but which basically pointed to the shifting borders
and blurring selves I've been harping on about.
I'm not sure what Basil would have made of Hopkins,
but I know he would like the part of the song where Phelps
sings, *let's dig a hole into an old book;*
keep our secrets there. Gouge away, I guess,
as if everything we had to hide were blessed.

❖

At the level of what I know empirically,
there still not much—maybe the way soup beans
or sesame start to dry as the season ends,
or how the fields put on their darker yellow
masks of mustard and ragweed and daisy-cousin
blossom. Though I don't know what all that means
other than a colder season coming.
It's not cold yet; we're still thanking summer
for its mercy, asking the just-ripe grapes to take
our thirst in bursts of juice from their split skins.
I like the way a muscadine is often
ugly and blotched on the outside, it makes
me think twice what sweetness might be worth,
that it sometimes doesn't come easily for even
the best of things—for vines or melodies
or men. *Come along to the riverside,*
lay down now, the song goes on, asking not
for conversion but just for quiet, *we can hold or not*
say all at all. Sometimes the silence in Basil's
letters, and between the letters, says as much
about the space communication requires,
or communion even, or community,
as the words he manages to scrape across
the page. *That I love you, learn from the letters I write*,
he writes, in grief, to an unknown accomplice.
That I love you, says this place, learn from the poplar
leaves that fall first and wither on the ground
and from the beech leaves that cling and shiver through

the hardest winds of winter. *That you hate me,*
I know from your silence. That you hate me I know
in the way you don't know the names of everything
that grows and dies here, the pale-blue, inch-high blossoms
in spring you claim to love, the impossibly pink
pin-flowers that hide behind the blackberries,
half the trees in the woods. *But write, at any rate,*
in the future, with pen and ink and a bit of paper
loving those who love you. But give me the feet
of your family, not just your lonely, predictable
feet, and love the things that love you, says
this place. One day I'll find a way to listen.
The sun is down, and half the world's asleep—
the killdeer, my kids, and all I've tried to keep.

VI

Monastery of the Holy Spirit

CONYERS, GEORGIA

Listen, child of God, to the almost nothing-
sound the turtle makes edging through
the pond that collects in the basin that the bottom
of the hill below the chapel makes, its whisper
more the echo of remembered rhyme
or a glad sound returning from another
time, some childhood sound, or maybe something
more basic even than that. Where my dad and I sat
beside the pond (before we'd climbed the hill
for midday prayers), we talked about the geese
that must be raising young and the woodpeckers
whose phone calls we could just make out, the snakes
we thought we'd seen cipher away as the trail
turned out ahead of us, and the heat, which weighed
on us and weighed us in survival's scales.
Conyers is about an hour southeast
of Atlanta, and the monastery, of course,
used to be in a happy rural seat, but the city
came to it, the way that southern cities do,
and is now still knocking on the door of the chapel
and the museum / visitors' center, begging

to be let in. So the pond below the church
has the feel of something planned but then forgotten,
a livestock pond for the ghost cattle of the fifties.
But it smelled like pine in the way that Georgia does,
and the heat merged with the borders of our bodies
in the way it does and stretched our senses of self,
or our selves became submerged and subliminal.
Mountains of the dead, are you listening?
Jason Molina sings in a song that seems
only about half-done, *you're going to lose*
a lot. The song was in my head while my dad
and I waited on a stone bench surrounded
by goose and duck droppings and martial files
of ants. We talked about recovery
and my brothers and the way the turtle is
a brother to the pond. From our low vantage
we couldn't see the monastery, so
there was, briefly, only Georgia in summer, and us,
bound by the faiths we put in family
and the heat, which felt for all the world like our breath,
or the world's breath, or some counterweight to death.

❖

Late in Basil's correspondences
with the world around him is a well-known set
of letters to Libanius, whose replies
are also included in the manuscript
tradition. Just when Libanius and Basil
might have met, or when the letters were sent, or if
they are even authentic is up for scholarly
debate. But reading Basil's arc of letters
through, and coming upon these almost trifling
parries of compliments and admiration
and friendship, one can't help but feel a kind
of gladness at the youthfulness of expression,
of what a friend will do to the way we see
ourselves, like the echo of remembered rhyme
somewhere caroling in our traitorous ears,
if by traitorous I really mean just truthful
in the way our lonelinesses get corrected.
You've already lost so much, Molina sings
in the song I mentioned, *now that the moon has passed
you by*. Of course the moon is never lonely
but beautiful in the way it stays alone
with us. There was something *indescribably
delightful in the language* of your letter,
Basil writes in reply to a similar assignation
of beauty from Libanius. Each friend
can't keep from praising the other's style. Like smiles
on faces translated and then moored to the page,
like the memory of a passing moon preserved.

It is the nature of words to disclose the love
that is within the soul; so says the final
letter in the sequence between these friends.
And the letter might be fake, or have been faked,
or be between two other distanced friends,
but the way it rings out like some kind of postlude
to the wrangling words on trinities and prayer,
widows, illnesses, and what spirits are
and are not there casts a kind of spell
backward over the world of Christian world-
making Basil's been engaged in. That in
the salvation of the self there must always be room
for love seems so obvious when I write it down—
last word: pure verb that is our densest noun.

❖

As with the echo of remembered rhyme,
the chapel felt at once newly lovely
and familiar. It didn't have air-conditioning
but was filled with afternoon darkness and a blue
light rivering through strange blue windows.
The brothers, when the church was built, received
dispensation from whatever hierarchy
loomed over them at the time to use stained glass.
They pointed out that the usual humility
of plain clear glazing would be too hot in Georgia,
so they learned the craft of window making and fit
the length of the choir with narrow, tall blue windows
and the altar at the back with yellow. My dad
pointed out the contrast, how you could barely see
through the blue, and we guessed they probably meant it that way.
All the good things are asleep in the human world;
it makes more room for the dark to walk around.
The architects agreed with Molina here
and let the darkness, whether it be by night
or not, stay dark. There were fans above our pews
and above the brothers' choir, so the prayers and psalms
were nearly drowned by noise, but maybe more so
drowned in the river here. I held my hand
up in the light and thought to ask my dad
if he could swim. I meant it as a joke,
but he might not have seen it that way. I am grateful
for his years of swimming and remembering
to breathe and the way he must have treaded water

for what felt like years at times. *You've already lost
so much*, he might have heard some mountain singing
last year when he nearly died, but he treaded light
for long enough to keep from losing more.
When we left the chapel after prayers, the blue
stayed in our eyes like sleep. The sun felt muted
like a muted trumpet, the trumpet vines along
a wall were drained of their August desire-color,
and the coin-flash god's winks in the pond between
the trees seemed more like signals in a fog—
some far-off trawler not communicating
but marking out with light its own existence
in the blueish mist, which also gave it form,
like a body embraced, a hold forevered and warm.

❖

Speak to all my friends, goes the line in the song
after the bit about the walking dark,
whose names I can't remember now. And it's
not clear if this is a command or missing
an *I'll*, which would make it more of an internal
reminder to right oneself when that becomes
more possible. And maybe in St. Basil's
back-and-forthing with Libanius
there's something of the suddenly remembered
name, at least for the reader. As I said, there's no way
to precisely date the letters, but coming on them
at the end one feels like Basil has remembered
friendship or friendship has remembered him
in a crucial way. Where do we add the human
to our gods? Is the spirit that connects us one
to one the same as Basil's holy one?
It seems to me that any mystery
of faith—friendship, family or then
forthrightness and forgiveness—depends, in ways,
on the same nameless confusion, the darkest shade
of the nearest woods. Our friends' names in our mouths
feel strange, our fathers' names across our teeth
are alien almost, like something said
for the first time every time you say it. Or, like
the echo of remembered rhyme, your ear
registers the sound while your mind repels it.
Well, not repels but has to reaffirm
commitment to it. I say "Kate" and my mind beholds

the mystery of love for a lover. I say
"Daddy" and my mind remakes the giving
of life that gave to him his shape and name.
Each time, with language and signification,
we create communities out of air and ear.
We are barely there. *My heart is sick, and I didn't
make it out*, he sings at the almost end of the almost-
song, but in our barely being we've defeated
death. I conjure your heart by saying it.
My father brings back his father. Remember *it is
the nature of words to disclose the love that is
within the soul*, writes Basil on the subject
of this magic, near the end of his own show;
we can only love what we know we do not know.

❖

Now back inside the chapel, if you'll forgive
the retreat, I wanted to think again about
the window-light. It is the principal
feature of the place, the one thing I'll
remember over any other—not the screen
door that wouldn't shut (appropriately,
we thought), not the creaking of the choir stalls,
or the saddle-stitched, careworn pamphlets of psalms, the alms
you could leave if you could leave them, the elegance
of arches, the march of souls constrained, maybe freed,
by form. Is this kind of light a lie? A dye
on experience and memory? Or is
there always a surface of charade or magic?
In Basil's last letter, he writes to Gregory,
his oldest friend, of a mutual acquaintance:
He who in our sight is a mimic actor,
but in yours a pious man, having come to us
on a propitious and brilliant day has departed
in a manner truly befitting a god. So the one
seems the other and then rhetorically is
another. Three in one. Community,
solitude, and self. We watch each other
walk away and also walk away ourselves.
Before we left the monastery, my dad
and I went to the gift shop for fudge to bring
back home (they also grow bonsai and, of course,
stain glass). We paid and I watched him move ahead
of me slow through the doors and into the heat

of the newly afternooned August light. His head
was bent but not in prayer. It was as if
subconsciously he'd been listening for the sound
of my feet behind him, where I was walking through
a strip of barely rooted sod (the visitors'
center is relatively new). Twenty
yards ahead he stopped to wait and turned
around. *This time*, sings Molina, *I'm leaving nothing
behind*, which maybe my dad was thinking too,
but I bet he was really just wondering where I'd gone.
We move together and we move apart,
our movements strangely familiar to each other,
like letters or a tune, or blue light, or time,
or like the echo of remembered rhyme.

ACKNOWLEDGMENTS

Section VI appeared in *Cincinnati Review*.

Lyrics from "Time of the Preacher" and "Denver" by Willie Nelson. Used with best intentions.

Lyrics from "Northstar Blues" by Jason Molina from *What Comes After the Blues* (Magnolia Electric Company). Copyright © 2005 by Autumn Bird Songs. Used by permission of Secretly Canadian Publishing.

Lyrics from "Everybody Will Be Happy Over There" by E. M. Bartlett, 1921.

Lyrics from "Paradise" by John Prine from *John Prine*. Copyright © 1970 Sour Grapes Music Inc. and Walden Music Inc. All rights reserved. Used by permission of Alfred Music.

Lyrics from "Crow's Nest" by Kelly Joy Phelps from *Tunesmith Retrofit*. Copyright © 2006 by Pilgrim's Way Publishing. Used by permission of Kelly Joe Phelps.

Lyrics from "In the Human World" by Jason Molina from *Sojourner* (Magnolia Electric Company). Copyright © 2007 by Autumn Bird Songs. Used by permission of Secretly Canadian Publishing.

All quotations from St. Basil's letters are from *Saint Basil: The Letters*, vols. 1–4, translated by Roy J. Deferrari. Loeb Classical Library, William Heineman, Harvard University Press, 1926.

Thanks to Jeff Vogel for reading. Thanks to Kelly Joe Phelps for the phone call.

And special thanks to Brother Paul Quenon, David George, Maurice Manning, and Tom Perry, without whom this poem could not have been made.

The Backwaters Prize in Poetry was suspended from 2005 to 2011.

To order or obtain more information on these or other University of
Nebraska Press titles, visit nebraskapress.unl.edu.